Evangelical Anglicans and The Lima Text:

An Assessment and Critique

drafted
on behalf of the Church of England Evangelical Council
by

Tony Price

Assistant Curate of St. Mary's, Wootton, Bedford and Minister in Charge of Stewartby United Church

GROVE BOOKS LIMITED
Bramcote   Nottingham   NG9 3DS

CONTENTS

FOREWORD

The 'Lima Text', *Baptism, Eucharist and Ministry* (W.C.C. 1982) will undoubtedly form a landmark in ecumenical discussion, and we are therefore glad to present this contribution to discussion and response to it. The Church of England Evangelical Coucil asked its Theology Group to draft a document to help towards an evangelical mind on the 'Lima Text'. They in turn invited Tony Price to work on this. His setting, as an evangelical Anglican minister working in a Local Ecumenical Project in Stewartby, near Bedford, gives him an appropriate background to comment on the Statement. Drafts of his document were considered at the Council's meetings in January and April 1985, and this booklet is now offered as a contribution to the Church's thinking on the 'Lima Text'.

Jill Dann
(Chairman of C.E.E.C.)

First Impression July 1985

ISSN 0144-1728

ISBN 1 85174 000 7

PREFACE

The ecumenical movement originally grew out of the determination of evangelicals at the end of the last century to see 'the evangelization of the world in this generation'. The formal beginnings of the movement can be traced to the International Missionary Conference held at Edinburgh in 1910; so it has its roots in a concern that the 'whole inhabited earth' (Greek *oikoumene*) may hear and believe this gospel of Christ. The work of that Conference was continued by three main thrusts: the International Missionary Council (formed in 1921), the Faith and Order movement (formed to discuss those things about which the churches differed; first World Conference, 1927), and the Life and Work movement (first conference in 1925, it aimed at creating a better social, economic, political and international order for the world). After the Second World War, 'Faith and Order' combined with 'Life and Work' to form in 1948 the World Council of Churches, and in 1961 the International Missionary Council also combined with the WCC.

The document *Baptism, Eucharist and Ministry* (which we shall refer to from now on as BEM) is itself not a recent development, but the fruit of a process of study and discussion begun at that first World Conference on Faith and Order (Lausanne, 1927). At first it was only the Protestant Chuches which were fully involved in the discussions, but since the WCC Fifth Assembly (Nairobi, 1975), there has been fuller active participation by both Roman Catholic and Eastern Orthodox theologians as well. Since 1979, the steering group responsible for BEM has been under the presidency of Frère Max Thurian of the Taizé Community.

BEM is known as 'the Lima Text' because it was at a plenary session of the Faith and Order Commission held at Lima, Peru, in 1982, that the final revision of the document received the Commission's unanimous approval, and was sent to the Churches with the request for their official response.

The wide involvement of theologians from such a broad spectrum of the universal Church means that the agreement expressed in BEM is all the more remarkable. It is not yet full consensus—that is, a unanimous agreement—but certainly shows a considerable 'growing together' in doctrine. It indicates that the Churches have much in common in their understanding of their faith; perhaps more than they thought; perhaps even enough to make possible some real further steps towards unity.

Certainly, at the time of writing the text has been referred by the General Synod to the dioceses of the Church of England along with the ARCIC *Final Report*, and it is now up to the Church of England at large to make a substantial response.

1. INTRODUCTION

1. A New Ecumenical Initiative

'The statement published here marks a major advance in the ecumenical journey.' This is the claim that has been made for BEM, but it may have a hollow ring for those people who feel that the ecumenical advance has become bogged down beyond hope of recovery. In 1982, the Proposals for Covenanting for Unity failed to receive the required majority in the Church of England's General Synod, and ever since then, many ecumenically-minded Christians have more or less given up hoping for unity at a central, denominational level. The failure of the Covenant caused a lot of hurt and bitterness among Free Church people, who felt rightly that they were making big concessions in the direction of the Church of England, only to find their sacrifice, and themselves, rejected. The pain of this 'kick in the teeth' is only just beginning to fade away, leaving an understandable wariness about further advances. Meanwhile, Anglicans working in Local Ecumenical Projects are often frustrated at having been 'let down by their own side', and there is a growing feeling among ecumenical colleagues that the official rules *must* be changed. It is good to see that, at the time of writing, the Church of England is taking some steps to effect these changes.[1]

At the same time as this continuing unrest and pushing at the limits, there is also a rather evil kind of blackmail going on, which aims to prevent many kinds of progress in the church on the grounds that it may prejudice unity. (This works both ways. 'If the Church of England ordains women it will make union with Rome impossible', can always be countered by 'We must not move too far towards Rome for fear of alienating our nonconformist brethren'.)

Yet it is just because ecumenical progress is at an impasse, that BEM represents such a major achievement. One criticism of previous ecumenical efforts was that they were not sufficiently theologically grounded, or that they tended to skate over the differences, or dodge the real issues, in order to achieve an outward, organizational unity. BEM adopts the different approach of seeking to provide a solid foundation for future unity, that is based on *doctrinal convergence* rather than on a mere willingness to overlook differences of practice.

In the three major areas of baptism, eucharist, and ministry, which are about not only the practice but also the very life and faith of the Christian Churches, BEM claims to have found enough agreement about what is believed and taught, to make a real (and not merely notional) unity possible.

[1] The 'Derby' working party on Local Ecumenical Development reported in Summer 1984, and in November 1984 the General Synod accepted the main proposals, and initiated legislation to give them effect. Their provisions both loosen the general ecumenical situation, and also enable a diocesan bishop to designate specific areas as 'Local Ecumenical Projects' where the rules governing forms of worship and interchangeability of ministers are further relaxed. The Measure and Canons passed their Revision Stage in Synod in July 1985, and should become law around 1987.

2. Aim and Purpose of BEM

BEM does not claim to be a complete theological treatment of baptism, eucharist and ministry, and we should not look for that sort of treatment, or judge BEM harshly because it does not say all that we would want to say about them. Instead, it tries to concentrate on 'those aspects of the theme that have been directly or indirectly related to the problems of mutual recognition leading to unity'.

Within this limitation, BEM's declared aim is 'to become part of a faithful and sufficient reflection of the common Christian Tradition on essential elements of Christian communion.' (page ix). This rather awkward phrase seems to mean that BEM wants to be accepted as part of the process of handing on the Christian faith in this generation. Is it being faithful in this task? This is the real gist of the first question we are being asked to think about. (See further in this section).

BEM is now being submitted to the Churches, with the request that the fullest discussion should be carried on at every level of the Churches, so as to involve the whole people of God in the 'spiritual process of receiving this text'.

Since this may be an unfamiliar idea, it is worth having a brief look at the idea of *'reception',* which has recently proved fruitful in ecumenical thinking about the Church. It is based on the notion that the great Councils of the Church which, in the first few centuries after Christ, formulated and expressed the doctrines of the Trinity, the Person and Natures of Christ, the Person of the Holy Spirit, and so on, did not carry on their deliberations in some kind of vacuum. They did not make their decisions in isolation, and then see those decisions become automatically binding on all Christians: the Councils themselves were a part of the life of the whole Church. As Christians thought and prayed, and the work of one Council was continued by others, the conciliar process was in this way prolonged and extended to those who were not actually present at the Council. This was a necessary part of the authentication of councils and their decisions; for the authority which the councils claimed did not become fully real until their decisions had been weighed against the Scriptures and the existing creeds and teachings of the Church. This was the process by which those 'Ecumenical Councils' were recognized as such by the wider Church.

We are now being invited to become involved in a similar process of 'receiving' BEM. The great thing about this is that theological agreement between churches and traditions is now being approached, not as a matter for theologians alone, but as something which concerns the ordinary faithful, the whole people of God. In view of recent experiences of the gulf that exists between some theologians and the 'person in the pew', this is a hopeful sign.

Some people have found that reading BEM, thoughtfully and prayerfully, really can be a spiritual process and a spiritual experience. In spite of its frequent density of style, we can even try to read it devotionally, to enrich our understanding of the means of grace in it. (It is in any case our hope that readers will base their decisions about BEM on their own study of the text itself, rather than on a reading of any appraisals of it!).

In the case of the Church of England, 'receiving the text' has already taken the form of discussions in General Synod, and it is now to be discussed in diocesan and deanery synods. But it is to be hoped that PCCs and other groups will also find ways of studying BEM and learning from it, and this would be most valuable if it could be done ecumenically. The questions which BEM itself asks us to consider may be expressed in this way:

1. Is this text true to the Christian faith as we have received it and now understand it?

2. What consequences will it have for our relations with other churches, especially those which accept the text?

3. How will the text affect our own worship, life and witness?

4. What suggestions can our church make towards the continuing work of Faith and Order (a project to find a common expression of the apostolic faith for today)?

The purpose of this present appraisal is to look at a number of the points discussed in BEM and comment on them in a way that will help members of deanery synods, PCCs and others to understand the Lima text better, and be able to answer some of the questions.

3. Attitudes and Approach

William Lazareth and Max Thurian have made the following claim for BEM; that 'the Lima Text in its entirety is based on the Word of God as contained in Scripture and as understood in the communion of the Church of all ages and all places.' One of the questions that must be asked is whether this claim is justified, for it is clear that some of the conclusions reached in BEM are different from the ways in which evangelicals have traditionally expressed their belief. BEM therefore challenges us to look again at our own interpretation of biblical teaching, at the same time as we weigh its statements.

The convergence seen in BEM has grown out of an intensive common study of the Bible and patristics (the theology of the early Christian 'fathers'), together with insights drawn from the liturgical revival of the twentieth century, and probably also from the charismatic movement. Chiefly, however, it turns again and again to Scripture as its starting point.

The advantage of this has been to make it possible to look back beyond the disputes and divisions of the past five centuries, to the common roots in Scripture and the early Church, which all Christians acknowledge.

The overarching concern behind this attempt is mission: that at this critical and dangerous moment in the history of the human race, the Body of Christ may be one, so that its mission to a lost world may be effective.

I believe that, because of BEM's scriptural basis and missionary concern, evangelicals of all people should approach the document in a positive spirit and look for its success in what it sets out to do.

2. BAPTISM

1. Introduction and General Comments

The section on baptism is the shortest of the three parts of BEM, though the pattern it follows is broadly similar to that of the other two parts. It begins with a statement about the institution of baptism (I), rooting it firmly in the life, death and resurrection of Jesus, stressing that it was an essential part of Christ's 'Great Commission' in Matthew 28.18-20, and has been the universal practice of Church since apostolic times. It then discusses the meaning of baptism (II) under a series of headings drawn from New Testament teaching and images. This is followed by a section (III) on the relations between baptism and faith, before the text ventures (in section IV) into some of the more controversial issues surround baptism, which divide 'believer-baptist' from 'infant-baptist' traditions. A final section (V) introduces some discussion of the ways in which baptism is to be celebrated.

The paragraphs of the text itself are accompanied by paragraphs of Commentary in italics. These are intended throughout BEM to draw attention to historical differences which have now been overcome in the formulation of the text, or to identify issues which are still in dispute, and which call for further research and efforts to find agreement. The status of the Commentary is sometimes confusing, as the precise purpose of it differs from section to section. Sometimes it sheds real light on the text, while at other times it seems to undo some of the good things in the text. We sometimes suspect that it has been used simply as a device to remove problems that are too difficult from the immediate area of debate, while keeping them somewhere in the air. At any rate, it is seldom dull (once we have penetrated the mass of verbiage!).

It is perhaps worth making clear that the scope of this text is not only 'baptism' as practised in the Anglican Church, but the whole process of Christian initiation, which for us would include confirmation as a subsequent experience, and for some parts of the Church, chrismation (anointing with oil). All these are included in what means by baptism, which is described in a thoroughly Christ-centred and Trinitarian way. The paragraphs on the meaning of baptism, and the different images used to describe it, could well supply material for a series of Bible studies or sermons on the New Testament teaching on the subject.

2. Baptism and Faith

One suspicion we might feel on first reading the text, is that it seems to describe baptism and its effects in rather mechanical terms, attributing to baptism itself some of what we would more often see as belonging to *faith* in Christ. (e.g. 'Baptism . . . unites the one baptized with Christ and his people' (2) . . . 'God bestows upon all baptized persons the anointing and the promise of the Holy Spirit . . .' (5))

It is, therefore, reassuring to turn to section III, ('Baptism and Faith'), and find very clearly stated that faith is essential if the salvation embodied and set forth in baptism is to be received. All churches acknowledge this, and that 'personal commitment is necessary for responsible membership in the body of Christ' (8). Without faith, we may conclude, baptism does not convey salvation.

But BEM reminds us that the faith which makes baptism effective is never a once-for-all experience, but needs to continue through the whole of life, and that baptism too is related to a life-long growth in Christian discipleship. In case we had any illusions about 'cheap grace' being all that the Christian needs, we are helpfully reminded of the ethical implications, and the call for personal sanctification, that baptism also entails (9-10).

The place of faith in relation to baptism is an important preparation for what follows, and we should bear it in mind throughout the discussion of different views about who may be baptized.

3. 'Infant Baptism' and 'Believers' Baptism'
The most difficult problem the commission faced in this part of BEM was surely the expression of some kind of convergence between 'infant baptist' and 'believer baptist' traditions. It is here (in section IV, A) that the text becomes controversial, and presents a challenge to members of both traditions.

The text takes the New Testament evidence as its starting point and states that, although infant baptism 'cannot be excluded', it was baptism upon personal profession of faith that was the norm. As Colin Buchanan points out in his Grove Booklet on ARCIC and Lima, (see bibliography), there is a much stronger case for infant baptism than this implies, and that case is based on the biblical evidence itself. We can afford to be confident in our belief that it is entirely appropriate to baptize the infant children of Christian parents, because we believe in God's covenant promises made first to Abraham, and fulfilled in Christ.

In describing the different kinds of baptismal practice that have grown up since apostolic times, BEM runs the risk of being merely descriptive: 'Some churches baptize infants . . . Other churches practise exclusively the baptism of believers . . . ' (11). The problem is that, while everyone must agree with this, their agreement with BEM would not bring them a step nearer to actual unity, or to agreement with each other about baptism itself.

But BEM does go further than this, by returning to the theme of the *faith* that is expressed in baptism, and stressing the importance of the *community* of faith.

There is no question in any tradition of wanting to separate baptism from faith. All traditions begin with the assurance that baptism is primarily about a gift from God, and then about a human response to it. Where infants are baptized, that personal response of faith and commitment must follow later in life. Where older persons are baptized on their own profession of faith, that too is not an end in itself, for a continuing growth of personal response and faith is expected just as much from them. The Commentary (12) points to the importance of the community of faith. In 'infant baptism', it is the faith of the Christian community, and particularly the parents, that is emphasized; but in 'believers' baptism', it is still within the community of faith that the individual makes his own confession of faith. Seen in this way, the difference becomes 'less sharp'. Even if this were not so, all the churches could gain by understanding faith in less 'individualistic' terms than in the past, and recapturing a vision for continuing Christian nurture and growth for all believers.

Following these comments, BEM makes the tentative suggestion (Commentary (12) and paragraph 15) that all the churches might adopt the practice of some churches which already unite both 'infant baptist' and 'believer baptist' traditions, by regarding to two patterns of entry into the Church as 'equivalent'.

Desirable as such a recognition might be, it is probably over-optimistic of BEM to suggest that it is likely in any but exceptional circumstances, and where the will to unity is already strongly present. Where that will is absent, the differences over baptism will be regarded as more fundamental: not as differences of practice, but as differences about the attitude towards authority, obedience to Scripture, and so on.

If the different traditions could agree to accept the proposals of BEM, what exactly would be involved for both 'sides'?

'Believer baptists' would need to recognize the baptism practised by 'infant baptists' as a valid baptism (and this is the apparently insurmountable obstacle); and would also need to refrain from any practice which might be interpreted as 're-baptism'.

On the other hand, churches which practise infant baptism would need to examine their own baptismal discipline, and refrain from the apparently indiscriminate baptism of children whose parents show no evidence of the faith in Christ which is supposed to be the basis for that baptism. This is just the sort of step that many in the Church of England already desire, and long to see official sanction for. Too many evangelical Anglicans have been tempted to abandon the Church's teaching on the fitness of infant baptism in favour of a Baptist position, because of their disgust with the actual practise of the Church. Putting our own house in order would not only stop the rot here, but also help to persuade Baptists that our baptism of the infant children of Christian parents is valid. We would also need to place greater emphasis on Christian nurture for the young (as well as for all believers), with a view to eliciting a mature response of faith later in life (16). This like the other challenges to us is more to be welcomed than feared.

4. The Problem of Confirmation
A further problem for Anglicans is raised by what looks like a devaluing of baptism, when we insist that a person must be confirmed before he or she can be considered a full member of the Anglican church, and admitted to communion.

This is not sufficiently dealt with in paragraph 14 on 'Baptism— Chrismation—Confirmation', where there is again a tendency merely to describe different forms of practice, rather than try to resolve those differences. The question is: where is the sign of the gift of the Spirit to be found, in Christian initiation? Is it in water baptism itself, in the anointing with oil (chrismation), or in the laying on of hands (confirmation)? As Colin Buchanan has said, we want to reject anything that smacks of 'two-staging', and stress that it is the single rite of water baptism itself which is the sign of the fulness of the gift of the Spirit.

If baptism alone is complete, then there are strong theological arguments for allowing every baptized person to take part in the eucharist. This would include admitting even children to the Lord's table, as the Orthodox do—without making any arbitrary distinctions about 'minimum age'. And BEM itself points out (Commentary (14)) the inconsistency of our failure to do this.[1]

Of course, not all evangelicals will agree with this. There are many who feel that the present Anglican discipline on admission to communion has got it just about right: it holds in balance the grace of God (which always comes first) with the response of faith (without which no one can be a Christian). But others regard confirmation as the 'lame duck' of Anglican practice. They find it absurd to insist on confirming people already baptized as adults, and wrong to submit to the pressure to confirm children and teenagers when they are really too young, just so that they can take their (rightful?) place with the church around the Lord's table. Admitting baptized children to communion would remove this pressure. Any form of service in which they later made a public profession of faith would then come to have a real significance, because it could wait until the mature personal commitment was really there. At any rate, BEM challenges us to have another try at re-thinking confirmation, so as to make it clear that there is no suggestion of 'completing' baptism, or 'topping-up' a partly-filled believer with the Holy Spirit.

If we accept BEM's challenges about this whole area of baptismal practice and discipline, it would well enrich our rites of Christian initiation, and tighten us up in places where we have for too long been pastorally and theologically slack.

---

[1] At the time of writing, the Church of England is about to receive strong recommendations from its own 'Knaresborough' working party to make this change.

3. EUCHARIST

1. General Outline

Like the text on Baptism, this statement begins with a very scriptural account of the institution of the eucharist (I), quoting the words of St. Paul in 1 Corinthians 11.23-25, and discussing the general significiance of meals in the life and ministry of Jesus. The meaning of the eucharist (II), although it is 'essentially one complete act', is for the sake of convenience discussed under five headings: as (A) thanksgiving to the Father, (B) memorial of Christ, and (C) invocation of the Holy Spirit (thus rooting the eucharist in the persons of God Himself, as Trinity); as (D) communion of the faithful (stressing that it is a common meal shared by the people of God—the 'horizontal' dimension); and lastly, (E) as 'meal of the Kingdom' (where the perspective is eschatological, i.e. looking towards the final consummation of God's Kingdom). The statement concludes with a section (III) on the celebration of the eucharist, which discusses the elements a eucharistic liturgy should include, and such issues as presidency, frequency of celebration, and what to do with the bread and wine after the celebration. (A new Christian might consider some of these issues trivial . . . but that is far from being the case, as a study of church history would soon show.)

One of the particularly striking things about this document is its *enthusiasm* for the eucharist. The emphasis throughout is that the eucharist is the central act of Christian worship, and as such, should be celebrated frequently—at least each Sunday. Every Christian should be encouraged to receive communion frequently. The document does indicate a high degree of agreement about the eucharist, and in this it owes a considerable debt to the Liturgical Movement, and the revized and reformed liturgies which many churches have adopted in the last few decades. It is hard to imagine that parts of this text would have been acceptable to many Protestants, fifty or even thirty years ago; and it seems that liturgy itself has been the great teaching and transforming medium that has done much to bring about the convergence expressed here.

2. The Presence of Christ in the Eucharist

Ever since the Reformation, and the Reformers' rejection of the doctrines of transubstantiation and the sacrifice of the Mass, one of the principal subjects of dispute over the eucharist has been the way in which the presence of Christ is to be understood. Is the eucharist 'merely' a memorial of Someone who is present in this act in just the same way as in any other act of Christian worship or fellowship? Or is there something so special about it, that Christ is present in a different way or to a greater degree, in connection either with the consecrated elements of bread and wine, or with the believers who receive those elements in faith?

BEM seeks to find a way through some of the thornier problems that have surrounded ecumenical discussion of the eucharist, by turning to recent thinking about the biblical idea of 'memorial'. (The New Testament Greek word is *anamnesis*, used by St. Paul in 1 Cor. 11.24

and 25). According to such studies, the biblical meaning of *anamnesis* was not just a subjective remembering, but a sort of 'concrete remembering', a bringing back out of the past into the present of the thing, event or person being remembered. (cf. A. G. Hebert in Richardson, *Theological Word Book of the Bible,* p.143). Jesus' words, 'Do this in remembrance of me' would, then, mean that the eucharist was to be a way of 'actualizing' the Sacrifice of Calvary, or indeed Christ himself, and making them present to those who celebrate the eucharist.

Christians in the Reformed traditions have tended to be suspicious of this kind of thinking. They fear that it denies the uniqueness of Christ's sacrifice, and opens the door to the medieval view that his sacrifice is offered anew each time the eucharist is celebrated—one of the very errors which the Reformers were most intent on correcting! It has been suggested that BEM has taken a wrong turning by stressing this particular aspect of *anamnesis.* Recent studies in liturgy have called it into question, suggesting that it cannot sustain the weight of interpretation is has sometimes been made to bear. To be fair to BEM, however, it is fairly moderate in its use of this idea of *anamnesis*, and does not follow it to mistaken extremes. While we might prefer to avoid this language altogether, we would not want to disagree with paragraphs 5's explanation of the memorial of Christ as 'the living and effective sign of his sacrifice'; that is, a means by which God's work accomplished in the past becomes fully effective today. It might also be worth thinking of other kinds of memorial, such as the Passover. This is not so much about making past events actual in the present, as about people in the present *identifying themselves* with the events of the past, so that the meaning and effect of those events become real for them.

It is really because the eucharist is a memorial of Christ that BEM is able to speak of his 'real presence' in this sacrament. It quotes Jesus' words, 'This is my body . . . this is my blood', and adds, 'What Christ declared is true, and this truth is fulfilled every time the eucharist is celebrated' (13). But at the same time, it must be confessed that 'Christ's mode of presence in the eucharist is unique.' BEM wishes to recognize Christ's presence, without trying to define the exact mode of it. Is it to be definitely linked with the bread and the wine, or not so definitely? (Commentary (13)) An excess of definition has often proved divisive in the Church, rather than wholesome; and it may well be that BEM is right in seeing the next step towards unity as being agreement about the fact of Christ's presence in the sacrament joined with a respect for other Christians' sincerely held different views about how he is present.

As evangelicals we would however want to argue for a stronger emphasis on the fact that the eucharist is primarily a memorial of the *death* of Christ. It is regrettable that paragraph 13 quotes only half of the words of institution, and does not emphasize 'This is my body *given* for you . . . This is my blood *shed* for you'. It is regrettable, too, that when BEM quotes 1 Corinthians 11.26 ('For as often as you eat this bread and drink the cup, you proclaim the Lord's *death* until he comes') it does so only with reference to the Second Coming. It does not take up the point that until that event, throughout the whole of history, it is the death of Christ that is being proclaimed.

We would also be concerned about the words in paragraph 32: 'Some churches stress that Christ's presence in consecrated elements continues after the celebration.' The words imply that Christ must first be present in a way that can be definitely linked with the elements, and this is more than we would be willing to say. But in view of what has already been said, this is probably not the 'official' view of BEM, but has the status of a description of what some Churches believe: one of the differences we are being asked to respect, without having to accept it ourselves.

3. The Notion of 'Sacrifice'

The biblical conception of memorial is also pressed into service to try to resolve some of the historical disagreements about whether the eucharist is to be understood as a 'propitiatory sacrifice', as Catholic theology has taught.

BEM is quite definite about the uniqueness, the unrepeatability, the 'once-for-allness' of the sacrifice of Christ, who now 'ever lives to make intercession for us'(8). The Commentary on paragraph 8 invites the Churches to see Catholic references to the 'propitiatory sacrifice' of the Mass in the light of this unceasing intercession: 'The understanding is that there is only one expiation, that of the unique sacrifice of the cross, made actual in the eucharist and presented before the Father in the intercession of Christ and of the Church for all humanity.' Colin Buchanan has drawn attention to the 'oddities' of the expressions 'made actual' and 'presented before the Father', which might be considered as leaning too far in their application of the 'memorial' language. Others might think (as the Commentary plainly invites them to), 'If this is all that is meant by the idea of "sacrifice" in this context, then perhaps it need not be so hated and feared as we formerly thought.' But this is one of the problems of using language which can carry so many different shades of meaning, depending on the tradition, experience and culture of those who use it. Even if we accept the use of the word 'sacrifice' as it is expounded here, we ought still to recognize that other people might use it to mean very different, and much less acceptable, things.

In any event, the explanation in question is part of the Commentary rather than the text, and so it rightly reminds us that the issue is still unresolved, and must be on the agenda for further discussion. The text itself is most careful to avoid any reference to sacrifice other than what we find echoed in Anglican liturgy: that 'the eucharist is the sacrament of the unique sacrifice of Christ' (8) and the Church's 'great sacrifice of praise' (4).

4. The Holy Spirit and the Eucharist

One of the strong points of BEM is the emphasis in the texts concerning baptism and the eucharist on the importance of the Word of God, and that there must be a right balance between Word and Sacrament. (e.g. *Baptism,* 20, 21; *Eucharist* 3, 12, 27)

But it may be the Orthodox Churches which have made a further valuable contribution to the text by stressing that the Holy Spirit also plays a vital part in the eucharist: he it is who makes the crucified and risen Christ really present to us (14), and it is by his power that the bread and wine become the sacramental signs of Christ's body and blood (15). The Orthodox have always laid great stress in their liturgies on the *epiklesis,* that is, the invocation of the Spirit on the community and on the elements of bread and wine: and more recently other Churches, including the Church of England, have made this invocation more explicit in their revised liturgies—though the Church of England stops short of a direct petition that the Spirit would come upon the elements.

This is not just a question of words, or of a rather unpractical theological doctrine. A renewed experience of the Holy Spirit, whether in charismatic renewal or in the church's sacramental life, can only make the eucharist become *more* real, and give an understanding of Christ's presence which unites people because it is a living experience, instead of dividing them because it is only a matter of theory. The Commentary (14, 15) certainly envisages that realizing the Holy Spirit's part in the eucharist in a new way will remove some of the differences concerning a special moment of consecration, and whether or not a change is wrought in the elements themselves. As with the question of Christ's presence, the churches may discover they can be united in spiritual experience before they find full agreement about the ways they describe that experience theologically.

5. Eucharist and Christian Unity

Every time that Christians celebrate the eucharist, they affirm that it is a sacrament not only of their union with Christ, but also of their unity with one another. 'Though we are many, we are one body, because we all share in one bread.' (cf. 1 Cor. 10.17) Yet this very act of the communion of the faithful is what has proved so divisive: a historical fact which is a scandal and a rebuke to all the Churches.

BEM, with its concern for Christian unity, rightly calls hypocritical and sinful any practice which denies any other Christian his share in the eucharist, or denies that other churches' celebrations of the eucharist are valid. The practice of the Church of England is to admit to communion members of other Christian churches 'who are in good standing in their own Church' (Canon B15A), but perhaps an acceptance of BEM would require some Anglicans to recognize more enthusiastically the validity of other Churches' ministries, and their celebrations of the eucharist. We may also need to consider whether we are not being inconsistent in refusing baptized children a share in the communion which is the right of Christians.[1]

On whether eucharistic intercommunion is a means to unity, or may only follow from it, see chapter 5 below.

6. Eucharist and World

If Christians spend a lot of time and energy discussing the subjects of Lima text, there is often criticism from inside and outside the Church, that time is being wasted on trivial, impractical, or merely 'domestic',

[1] But see above pp.9-10.

issues, which could be devoted to the real problems facing the world. BEM, however, stresses that Christian practice in all these areas is firmly rooted in the real world, for in particular, 'the eucharist embraces all aspects of life' (20), and calls us to a ministry of reconciliation, and full involvement in the continuing redeeming work of God in history. There is a lot of concentrated material in paragraphs 19 to 26 of this text, from which many congregations could well learn, and which would shake many out of their Christian complacency. For we are reminded that the eucharist is not only a transaction between an individual and his God, but has social, economic and political implications as well!

Once or twice, the document uses language which may be unfamiliar to evangelicals, stating that, in the eucharistic thanksgiving, 'the Church speaks on behalf of the whole creation' (4, 23), 'the world which God has reconciled is present at every eucharist . . . The eucharist thus signifies what the world is to become: and offering an hymn of praise to the Creator.' (4) In connection with this, 'the bread and wine, fruits of the earth and of human labour, are presented to the Father in faith and thanksgiving'. Colin Buchanan has drawn attention to this suspicious hint of a lurking 'offertory' theology (an idea—not so fashionable nowadays as it was—that the elements are an 'offering' made to God, rather than, as we would say, a gift of God to the church.) But he calls this 'a very minor blemish'. In any case, the main emphasis of BEM is that the 'direction' of the eucharist is from God to man; it is a gift from the Lord (1, 2, etc.); nevertheless, a gift which we still need to 'unpack' more and more, to enrich our appreciation of it.

7. Some Questions of Practice

Although evangelicals have always been enthusiastic about the eucharist, and recognized it as one of the most important means of grace, we must also confess that we have lagged behind other sections of the church in acknowledging its centrality in our worship. Perhaps we have sometimes had good cause. The preaching of the Word at parish communion may have suffered in quantity (but, in some cases, that may be no bad thing! And a concern for improved *quality* is more important.) There may have been some tendency to take communion too lightly and carelessly, because of its frequency. But any good and healthy step forward involves some risk or danger, and now we have some catching up to do.

BEM calls for a renewal of the eucharist (28), inviting churches to re-examine their liturgy and practice in the light of the present ecumenical agreement about it. This renewal would involve the celebration of the eucharist 'at least every Sunda' (31) as 'the central act of Christian worship' (1); a practice which many but not yet all churches follow.

It is probably not within the scope of BEM to discuss the problems which this might cause, problems which explain the fears felt by many people that the church might become a 'eucharistic sect'. But we should at least bear some of those problems in mind. One is, the difficulty of providing enough clergy to celebrate the eucharist in many small country parishes, with the result that there is sometimes no service at all. Another objection arises because Sunday worship is also an occasion for evangelism; and knowing the service will be eucharistic may deter the less fully committed from attending worship at all. Is there to be no 'half-way house' for the interested not-quite believer?

On the disposal of the consecrated bread and wine remaining at the end of communion, BEM asks the churches to respect the practice and piety of other Christians regarding the practice of 'reservation' of the elements. But it does urge that the main reason for reserving the elements is to distribute them to the sick, and apart from this, the most respectful way of dealing with them is to consume them reverently at the end of the service. In view of the increasing practice of extended communion, this need not cause any dissension. For the purpose of the communion of the sick, it is appropriate to retain the elements instead of consuming them immediately. But evangelicals will still want to take issue with any practice which makes the elements themselves an object of worship, and this seems to be the implied thrust of BEM as well.

8. Summing Up

The text on the eucharist is, all in all, an exciting statement which, in spite of occasional denseness, communicates an enthusiasm for this one liturgical act left to us by our Lord himself. A study and application of it could enrich our own devotional and church life; and though it will not in itself bring about Christian unity, it is encouraging to see such a degree of ecumenical convergence, which is in a real sense an expression of a growing towards consensus.

4. MINISTRY

1. Outline and Approach

The document on ministry is by far the longest of the three sections of BEM (—more than twice the length of 'Baptism'). Much of what it says may seem unnecessary or self-evident to someone used to an Anglican evangelical environment; so we should remind oursleves that not everyone will have shared our experiences or expectations of ministry. The Faith and Order Commission saw the ministry as 'the most delicate and controversial' of the issues with which they were dealing. We can see why, when we reflect that the Proposals for Covenanting for Unity foundered mainly because of problems about the mutual recognition of ministries; and, perhaps even more significantly, that it is in the House of Clergy of General Synod that the greatest opposition to the Covenant, and to other proposals such as that for the ordination of women, has been found.[1] Whether it is simply that the clergy feel their status is threatened by changes in ministry, or whether there really are more reputable, theological issues at stake, BEM is at great pains to see any differences in the most sympathetic possible light, and to try to deal with the real theological problems. The principal routes by which it hopes to find a way forward, are via convergence about the idea of *episkope* (that is, 'oversight' in the church), the charismatic dimension of ministry, and above all by an emphasis on *service,* (which is what 'ministry' really means!)

The general outline of the text is somewhat different from those on baptism and eucharist. It begins, very encouragingly, with a meaty section (I) on the church (the 'whole people of God'), and on its calling and purpose. Only then does it turn to consider the place of ordained ministry within the church: its biblical basis, function, and authority (II). The major issues surrounding ministry (from the point of view of moving towards unity) are then examined in three different sections. They are: the forms that ordained ministry should take (III); the questions of apostolic tradition and apostolic succession (IV); and ordination itself—what it means, how it is carried out, and what conditions are necessary (V). Finally, section VI looks at the issues that remain to be agreed in the progress towards the mutual recognition of ordained ministries, and at the steps which may need to be taken by the different churches.

2. The Ordained Ministry and the Whole People of God

The introductory section on 'The Calling of the Whole People of God' is one of the most helpful parts of this document. It makes it clear from the outset, that when we speak of 'ministry', we are speaking of the function of the whole church, not just of one special part of it. This theme is enlarged upon in terms of God's will that the whole of humanity should hear and respond to his call; so the church is the community of those who have already responded to it, and now bear witness to the rest of the world. The church's life is based entirely on the finished work of Christ; and is lived now in the power of the Holy

[1] These lines are penned on the eve of the new elections to General Synod in September 1985.

Spirit. The church's task is both to proclaim the Kingdom of God, and to be an illustration of it. In order for this task to be fulfilled, 'the Holy Spirit bestows . . . diverse and complementary gifts': the emphasis is on the need for every member of the church to identify and use his or her gifts, for building up the church and serving the world.

So far, the description has been of a general understanding of the people of God that is agreed by all the churches (though many congregations and individual Christians would benefit from reflecting on these principles more deeply, and applying them a lot more!). But the churches differ in their understanding of how to order church life, and it is here that we find differences about the role of the ordained ministry. In keeping with the ecumenical intention of this document, one of the central aspects of that role is to be a focus of the Church's unity (8). This may be an idea that some people will have to take 'on faith'. Church history and experience certainly do show that the authority of a properly ordained ministry has often kept the Church together, and prevented people from breaking away and starting groups based on their own private interpretations. But it must also be the case that the weaknesses or shortcomings of the ordained ministry have occasionally driven sincere Christians out of the church, to form their own churches and ordain their own ministers. Nevertheless, the fact that most churches do practise some form of ordination is an indication of its importance for church life and order. What is less certain, is whether it is true to say that the ordained ministry 'is *constitutive* for the life and witness of the church' (8). Does BEM mean that no church can function without an ordained ministry? Or is it even saying that it is the ordained ministry which brings a church into being? Some kind of leadership is certainly necessary, and whether it is called 'ordained' or not, it needs to be recognized by the church. But we should prefer to say that the ordained ministry arises out of the life of the church and exists for the whole church—not the other way round! There seems to be an ambiguity here which BEM fails to resolve fully.

BEM is good in its treatment of the responsibility of ordained ministry—building up the church by a ministry of Word and sacrament, and guiding it in its worship, mission and service (13)—and its authority. The nearest we get to a definition at this point is that ordination is 'essentially a setting apart with prayer for the gift of the Holy Spirit' (15). Because of this, the authority of the ordained ministry is to be seen not as a possession but as a gift. Words like co-operation, interdependence, and reciprocity, are used, to describe how authority is to relate to the believing community (16). Moreover, authority in the church can only be authentic if it conforms to the model of Christ, whose life was above all a life of service (cf. Mk. 10.45).

3. Ordained Ministry and Priesthood

Evangelicals have traditionally disliked the use of the word 'priest' to describe any ordained minister, on the grounds that it carries certain connotations of sacrifice, particularly in connection with the eucharist, which detract from the uniqueness of Christ's sacrifice. They have preferred to speak of the 'priesthood of all believers', which expressed the biblical theme that the Church is called to be a 'royal priesthood' (1 Peter 2.9; Rev. 1.6; 5.10).

The term BEM prefers to use for the second order of ordained ministry (which our own Ordinal calls 'priests') is 'presbyters'—a more literal translation from the NT Greek *presbuteros* (='elder'), and the alternative title used in the ASB Ordinal. But there is a paragraph (17) which tries to explain why some churches use the word 'priest'. All Christians are related to the priesthood of Christ and to the priesthood of the church. But in addition to this, ordained ministers 'may appropriately be called priests because they fulfil a particular priestly service by strengthening and building up the royal and prophetic priesthood of the faithful . . .'

Some might feel that the paragraph is not long enough to do justice to the problems. As it stands, it is rather like the treatment of sacrifice and the eucharist (see above, pages 12-13): it is all right, if this is all that is meant by it, but we ought to be wary of going very much further.

However, the purpose of BEM is to be a convergence document, expressing no more than that with which all the churches can agree. To this extent, there is nothing here for us to dissent from, and what other Christians might wish to add to BEM is outside the terms of the present consideration.

4. The Ministry of Women

Another thorny issue between the churches (and within our own) is the question of the ordination of women. BEM bases its discussion of this on the argument that Christ has broken down all human barriers, to create a new humanity in which 'there is neither Jew nor Greek, there is neither slave nor free, there is neither male nor female' (Gal. 3.28). Because of this, there is a need for a comprehensiveness in ministry, making full use of the varied and complementary gifts of both women and men. But then BEM is content merely to describe the different conclusions which the churches draw from this (Commentary (18) and paragraph 55), and urge that while further study and agreement are still necessary, the present differences need not be a barrier to the mutual recognition of ministries. This may be true and highly desirable; perhaps it is also worth pointing out that although BEM appears to sit on the fence about this question, its own logical conclusions seem to point towards the ordination of women. For example, paragraph 50 tells us that no one should be excluded from ordination on the grounds of handicap, race, or social class. 'Or of sex', seems to cry out to be added, especially when we remember paragraph 18. This may seem to be reading too much between the lines, and even if it is true, it is clear that not everyone in the Church of England will agree. Although the Anglican Evangelical Assembly in January 1983 took a 'straw poll' that was in favour of ordaining women to the presbyterate, there is far from universal agreement among evangelicals about this. Yet BEM makes no reference at all to those texts about authority and headship, on which evangelicals opposed to the ordination of women have tended to base their objection (e.g. 1 Tim. 2.11-12). It bases its position instead on general principles about the church and its ministry; and if those general principles are correct, then the ordination of women to the presbyterate would be a logical expression of the fulness of ministry.

5. The Threefold Ministry

'It is evident unto all men diligently reading holy scriptures and ancient Authors, that from the Apostles' time there have been these Orders of Ministers in Christ's Church; Bishops, Priests, and Deacons.' So begins our Ordinal: but the divided state of the Church about this indicates that it is by no means as evident as all that!

BEM, starting with the New Testament, notes that there is no single pattern of ministry described there, that may serve as a blueprint for all times. What there is, is a variety of forms, adapted for particular places and circumstances. However, it was a threefold pattern of bishop, presbyter and deacon, which became established as the norm during the first few centuries.

One of the surprises of the present-day ecumenical movement, is that it has become so enthusiastic about this threefold ministry. For example, BEM notes that the church may adapt its ministry to the needs of its situation, and that the Holy Spirit has often blessed other forms of ordained ministry; but then it goes on to recommend this particular pattern: 'the threefold ministry of bishop, presbyter and deacon may serve today as an expression of the unity we seek and also as a means for achieving it' (22).

In order to disarm the possible suspicions of non-episcopal churches, BEM qualifies this in a number of ways. All ministry should be exercised in a personal, collegial and communal way (26). This expresses the different insights of churches which are respectively more 'episcopal', more 'presbyterian', or more 'congregationalist'. The threefold pattern should never be so rigid that it hinders the special ministry of prophetic or charismatic leaders, which God often gives to challenge or awaken the church (33). There must be no suggetion that other patterns of ministry are, or have been, or will be, invalid (38). It is simply that, in the interests of unity, the threefold pattern may have a 'powerful claim to be accepted by' those Churches which do not already have it.

In case we in the Church of England feel at this point that we are having it all our own way, BEM goes on to challenge us as well. The threefold pattern is clearly not perfect. It needs reforming if it is to enable the church to witness most effectively (24-25). In particular, the order of deacons needs to revitalized, so that it is no longer just a stepping-stone towards the presbyterate, but a valuable order of ministry in its own right, with special responsibility for representing the church 'in its calling as servants in the world' (31). We need to adopt more of the insights of the collegial and communal dimensions of ministry, as well as the personal dimension (26). We need to be more flexible. And of course, we need to accept the criticism that if bishops are, as we have sometimes claimed, a focus of unity, then how is it that we are not in unity with other episcopal churches (38)? That unity also is something we must desire and be working for.

Again, most of these are challenges to reforms that many evangelicals would welcome and have long been looking for anyway.

6. Apostolic Tradition/Apostolic Succession

To some Christians (expecially Roman Catholics, and 'Catholic' Anglicans), it is important to believe that the form of episcopacy they enjoy is derived from the apostles in direct and continuous succession. They hold that the only valid orders or ministry are those which are within this 'apostolic succession'. Now it is very doubtful whether such a continuity really exists anywhere—certainly in terms of a direct succession of 'laying on of hands'—and the dividedness of the church would in any case call its authenticity seriously into question.

BEM tries to reconcile these differences by making a distinction between apostolic tradition and apostolic succession: 'Apostolic tradition in the Church means continuity in the permanent characteristics of the Church of the apostles': the apostolic faith, preaching the Gospel, the sacraments, transmission of the ministry, service and mission etc. (34). We look in vain for some explicit reference in this paragraph to the canon of Scripture as being an essential part of the apostolic tradition; perhaps we are supposed to feel it is implied in all that is said . . . *Within* this apostolic tradition, the apostolic succession of the ministry 'serves the continuity of the Church in its life in Christ and its faithfulness to the words and acts of Jesus transmitted by the apostles' (Commentary (34)).

The important thing is *continuity.* The church today has to be seen to be in continuity with the church of apostolic times; but that continuity is in and through history. BEM therefore stresses the importance of the orderly transmission of the ordained ministry, as the way of preserving the apostolic faith and helping the Church to live it out today. There are really two things at issue here. One is the continuity of the organization called 'the church'; the other is its fidelity to the faith of the apostles. If we had to choose which was the more important, we would say it is the present fidelity to the apostolic faith that really matters. But the point BEM makes is that the continuity of the organization has been the greatest safeguard of that fidelity. No one is really foolish enough to believe that Christianity 'fell out of the sky' in recent times—but many of today's house churches, and even many evangelical Christians, sometimes behave as if it had, and attach little value to the institutions of the church, or the 'orderly transmission' of its ministry. The historical continuity of the organization, as long as it is accompanied by a constant willingness to be reformed, ought to be appreciated more, as a guarantee that the shape and content of gospel and faith have been retained. And the authority enshrined in the church ought to be given greater weight that of purely personal interpretations and opinions.

With regard to unity, BEM points out that this continuity of apostolic tradition can be seen in all the main churches, even those which do not have bishops. The reality of 'oversight' in the church is there, even where the title of 'bishop' is not (37). Because this is the case, some non-episcopal churches are increasingly willing 'to appreciate the episcopal succession as a sign, though not as a guarantee, of the continuity and unity of the Church' (38), and to accept that succession into their own church order.

This will not present any problems for evangelical Anglicans. We have often 'sat light' to our bishops, and perhaps we ourselves need to come to see them as rather more important for the life of the church than we have done! But there may still be suspicions among Catholics about recognizing the apostolic tradition of non-episcopal churches, and fears and doubts among nonconformists about accepting episcopacy. As people who are 'standing in the middle', we have the privilege of being able to pray for and encourage both groups.

7. Mutual Recognition of Ordained Ministries

This is the vital next step of the ecumenical journey, towards which the whole of BEM has been directed. But it cannot come about without deliberate efforts, on the part of all the churches, to look at the practices of other Christians with a view to sympathy and understanding, and to look critically at their own practices, with a view to renewal and reform.

The issue of apostolic succession remains important, but 'Churches in ecumenical conversations can recognize their respective ordained ministries if they are mutually assured of their intention to transmit the ministry of Word and sacrament in continuity with apostolic times' (52). If this is to be the main criterion, it implies that there should be few problems about recognizing the ministries of other Churches with which the Church of England has been engaged in conversations.

Paragraph 53(a) describes what steps we in the Church of England may need to take. We must recognize the 'apostolic content' of the ordained ministry of non-episcopal churches, and that a ministry of *episkope* (i.e. 'oversight') does exist in those churches, in various form. We must also look carefully at out own understanding of the threefold ministry, and be prepared to make changes in it where the demands of mission make it necessary. In the light of the Tiller Report, the decline in numbers of ordination candidates, our continued dithering about ordaining women, and the loss of any distinctive and meaningful use of the diaconate, the renewal of the ministry is very much a live issue in the Church of England. The need for it may well stimulate us and urge us on as we look at the possibility of recognizing other Churches' ordained ministries.

5. CONCLUSION—A PERSONAL VIEW FROM THE ECUMENICAL FRONT

This booklet is only one evangelical contribution to the debate about BEM, and I have referred to some others in the bibliography.

On a personal level, my desire has been very much to commend BEM and not condemn it. I believe that it really is firmly based upon the Word of God, as it claims to be, and that its concern for church unity is a concern that Christian mission may be effective, 'so that the world may believe'. There may be certain emphases in BEM, or forms of expression, that do not come very naturally to evangelicals; but I hope the way I have explained those points has shown that there is little for us to fear in the way BEM expresses them. On the other hand, there are a great many exciting and positive things in the Lima Text which we can welcome willingly and joyfully. Many of the 'challenges' addressed to the churches—particularly the Church of England—are aimed at abuses or flaws which evangelicals have long been concerned about or wanted to rectify. For this reason it can be our hope and prayer that the Church of England will indeed accept the Lima text; and even more, that it will apply its suggestions.

BEM is only a step—though a highly significant one—towards full consensus among the Churches. Consensus of that order is seen as 'a gift of the Spirit' which is realized as a communal experience before it can be articulated by common efforts into words. Full consensus can only be proclaimed '*after* the churches reach the point of living and acting together in unity' (page ix, my italics).

The question is: are mutual recognition of ministries, and and some degree of intercommunion, a *means* towards fuller unity; or may they only *follow from* the completest possible doctrinal agreement? The Roman Catholic position has always been that there can be no unity without doctrinal agreement. And surprisingly, evangelicals have often tended to agree with them—at least about this point! But might it not be more fruitful to see Christian unity as an *organic* thing?—namely, that it is by living, and worshipping, and working, together with other Christians, that we may hope to grow into unity with them, in Christ and by the power of the Holy Spirit.

This is certainly the emphasis of the New Testament, which speaks of unity as something to which Christians *attain to* as a result of the whole church's ministry of building up the body of Christ (Eph. 4.13). It also speaks many times of unity as a treasure to be prized and worked for above almost all other goods. We may have to give up our own cherished opinions, practices, and preferences—everything that constitutes 'having our own way'—but any amount of such personal loss is preferable to dividing the Church. (Rom. 14-15; 1 Cor. 6 and 8; Eph. 4; Phil. 2) Yet the thrilling experience of many Christians in Local Ecumenical Projects and united Churches has been that the loss of 'one's own way' is slight, compared with the reward and the joy of sharing life with Christians from other traditions. Such sharing leads to deeper understanding of each other and of Christ, and to genuine love. It is indeed by agreeing to live and work together that we find our differences becoming smaller and ourselves growing together.

This is the approach of *BEM:* that the convergence expressed in the document is enough for us to agree to live, worship and work together as Christians, in faith and hope that this will lead us on the full unity and consensus. And so we shall see fulfilled Paul's prayer in Romans 15.5-6: 'May the God who gives endurance and encouragement give you a spirit of unity among yourselves as you follow Christ Jesus, so that with one heart and mouth you may glorify the God and Father of our Lord Jesus Christ.'

APPENDIX 1: FOR FURTHER READING

From an evangelical viewpoint:
References to Colin Buchanan are all to his Grove Booklet, *ARCIC and Lima on Baptism and Eucharist* (Worship Series No. 86).

David Wright's *Baptism, Eucharist and Ministry: An Evangelical Assessment* (Rutherford House Forum Paper 3; available from Rutherford House, Edinburgh, EH6 0JR) is a more critical appraisal of BEM, from a Scottish, and non-episcopalian, evangelical point of view.

Roger Beckwith has written a review of BEM published as Latimer Memorandum No. 7 (available from Latimer House, 131 Banbury Road, Oxford), and an article entitled 'The ecumenical quest for agreement in faith', on BEM and two other unity documents, in *Themelios* Vol. 10, No. 1 (Sept. 1984), (obtainable from UCCF, 38 De Montfort Street, Leicester LE1 7GP). Both of these adopt a more critical stance towards BEM.

Other fairly accessible works:
Two study guides are:
Baptism, Eucharist and Ministry. Seven Studies by John Matthews (B.C.C.) This is intended to be a 'popular' study guide, and includes the text of BEM, but not the Commentary.

Growing Together in Baptism, Eucharist and Ministry by William Lazareth (W.C.C.). This is the 'official' study guide.

For an Anglican discussion, see *Towards a Church of England Response to BEM & ARCIC* (GS 661), published by C.I.O.

Only for the very keen are works like,
Ecumenical Perspectives on Baptism, Eucharist and Ministry, edited by Max Thurian (W.C.C.): a volume of theological essays providing fuller treatment of some of the more technical issues behind BEM.

APPENDIX 2: DISCUSSION QUESTIONS

The aim of discussion of BEM should be to answer the questions set by itself (see page 6). These questions are offered only as suggestions, in the hope of making that eventual aim more attainable.

General

1. To what extent do you agree with the claim that 'BEM is based in its entirety on the Word of God'? Where BEM's use and interpretation of the Bible is different from yours, why is that?

2. What are the aims (both short- and long-term) of the ecumenical movement, as expressed in BEM? Where do those aims figure in your scale of Christian priorities?

3. What degree of doctrinal agreement is necessary before you can be in full communion with another Christian? Is that degree of agreement present *within* the Church of England, say?

Baptism

4. Does a person have to be baptized to be a Christian? How does your answer relate to what BEM says about the meaning of baptism, and the relation between baptism and faith?

5. Is water-baptism complete, or is some other rite necessary for full Christian initiation? What should confirmation mean; and what does it mean?

6. What changes in the way the Church of England does baptisms would be necessary or desirable as part of unity moves towards (a) Baptists, (b) Roman Catholics, (c) Eastern Orthodox?

Eucharist

7. What is the eucharist a memorial of, and what do you mean by 'memorial'? How is Christ present in the eucharist?

8. Can you accept BEM's explanation of the notion of sacrifice in the eucharist?

9. Do you agree that the eucharist should become the central act of Christian worship each Sunday? What might be the consequences of applying this throughout the Church, and are they acceptable?

Ministry

10. How much is the threefold pattern of ministry really a focus for unity, and a guarantee of our historical continuity with the apostolic faith? How could it be reformed, to meet the demands of mission in the 1980's?

11. What would you say to a doubting non-episcopalian, to persuade him that bishops are a good thing?

12. How must we change our patterns of ordained ministry so that they will really express the 'wholeness' of the spiritual gifts for ministry, given to the whole people of God?

STOCK LIST—GROVE BOOKLETS ON MINISTRY & WORSHIP [Nos. 1-70]
and GROVE WORSHIP SERIES [71 onwards]

The Worship Series (of 24 pages each) is now published four times a year. All titles cost **85p**. Numbers not included below are out of print. Asterisked titles are in a second edition or reprint

- *12. **The Language of Series 3** by David L. Frost
- *13. **What Priesthood has the Ministry?** by J. M. R. Tillard
- *14. **Recent Liturgical Revision in the Church of England Down to 1973** by Colin Buchanan (36 pages) **(£1.70)**
- 14A. **Supplement for 1973-4 to Recent Liturgical Revision in the Church of England** by Colin Buchanan
- 14B. **Supplement for 1974-6 to Recent Liturgical Revision in the Church of England** by Colin Buchanan
- 14C. **Supplement for 1976-8 to Recent Liturgical Revision in the Church of England** by Colin Buchanan
- 14D. See Liturgical Study 39 **(£1.70)**
- 15. **Institutions and Inductions** by Trevor Lloyd
- 16. **Alternative Eucharistic Prayers** by Derek Billings
- *20. **A Case for Infant Baptism** by Colin Buchanan
- *24. **Infant Baptism Under Cross-Examination** by David Pawson and Colin Buchanan
- 29. **The Ordinal and its Revision** by Peter Toon
- 30. **Liturgy and Creation** by Peter R. Akehurst
- 32. **Inaugural Services** Edited by Colin Buchanan
- 34. **Modern Roman Catholic Worship: The Mass** by Nicholas Sagovsky
- *35. **Drama in Worship** by Andy Kelso
- 40. **Freedom in a Framework: Some Possibilities with Series 3** by Richard More
- *42. **Christian Healing in the Parish** by Michael Botting
- 43. **Modern Roman Catholic Worship: Baptism and Penance** by Nicholas Sagovsky
- *44. **Exorcism, Deliverance and Healing: Some Pastoral Guidelines** by John Richards
- 49. **Prophecy** by David Atkinson
- 50. **Evangelicals, Obedience and Change** by Trevor Lloyd
- 52. **Inter-Faith Worship?** by Peter Akehurst and Dick Wootton
- 53. **Penance** by David Gregg
- 54. **Celebrating Christmas** by Richard More
- *55. **Urban Church Growth: Some Clues from Britain and South America** by Eddie Gibbs
- 56. **The Eastern Orthodox Liturgy** by John Fenwick
- *58. **Ministry to the Sick: An Introduction** edited by David Gregg (second edition due, 1985)
- 60. **Liturgy for Ordination: The Series 3 Services** by Michael Sansom
- *61. **One Baptism Once** by Colin Buchanan
- *62. **Preaching at Funerals** by Ian Bunting
- *64. **Grow Through Groups** by Eddie Gibbs
- 65. **Liturgy for Initiation: The Series 3 Services** by Colin Buchanan
- 66. **Encountering Westindian Pentecostalism: its Ministry and Worship** by John Root
- 67. **How Do Congregations Learn?** by David Gillett
- 68. **Liturgy for Communion: The Revised Series 3 Service** by Colin Buchanan
- 69. **The Attractive Church** by Kenneth White
- 70. **Preaching at Baptisms** by Gordon Ogilvie
- 71. **A Hymn Book Survey 1962-1980** by Robin A. Leaver
- 72. **A Late-Night Service: Compline in Modern English** by Mark Davies (also an offprint of the service)
- 73. **Family Festivals: An Approach to Worship in the Home** compiled by Michael Vasey, Tom Jamieson, Lyn Jamieson, Dan Young and Sue Young
- 74. **Pr**
- 75. **C**
- 76. **Le**
- 77. **In**
- 78. **Pr**
- 79. **Pr**
- 80. **Th**
- 81. **H**
- 82. **Eu**
- 83. **Re**
- 84. **Li**
- 85. **W**
- 86. **Al**
- 87. **In**
- 88. **W**
- 89. **Pre**
- 90. **Evangelical Anglicans and Liturgy** by Colin Buchanan
- 91. **Adult Baptisms** by Colin Buchanan
- 92. **Evangelical Anglicans and The Lima Text** drafted by Tony Price

ISSN 0144–1728   **ISBN** 1 85174 000 7

GROVE BOOKS LIMITED
RIDLEY HALL ROAD, CAMBRIDGE CB3 9HU
Tel: 01223 464748   Fax: 01223 464849

Printed by Hassall & Lucking Ltd., Cross Street, Long Eaton, Nottingham NG10 1HD   Tel. L.E. 733292